30 Bible Art Coloring DIY Bookmarks

Bible Verse & Mandala Coloring Bookmarks

This is the day the Lord has made; Let us rejoice and be glad in it

Psalm 118:24

I WILL PRAISE THEE WITH WHOLE HEART

PSALM 138:1

Join Us >> bit.ly/get_sample_free

Get Free "Reviw Copies" of our New releases
Exclusive offers and book giveaways
More events from our community

Thank you

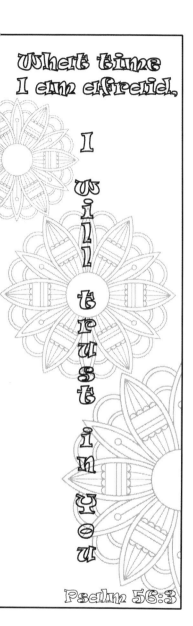

What time
I am afraid,
I will trust in you

Psalm 56:3

This is the day

the Lord
has made;

Let us rejoice

and

be glad in it

Psalm 118:24

Your word is a lamp to my feet and a light for my path

Psalm 119:105

Give thanks to the Lord, for he is good. His love endures forever

Psalm 136:1

Do to others
as
you would have
them do
To you

Luke 6:31

I CAN DO
EVERYTHING
THROUGH
HIM
WHO GIVES
ME
STRENGTH

PHILIPPIANS 4 13

I WILL

PRAISE THEE

WITH

MY WHOLE HEART

SALM 138:1

I AM THE GOOD SHEPHERD

JOHN 10:11

Children, obey your parents in the Lord, for this is right

Ephesians 6:1

EVERY WORD OF GOD PROVES TRUE

PROVERBS 30:5

You shall love

your neighbor

as

yourself

Matthew 22:39

Whatever
you do,

do everything

for

the glory
of God

1 Corinthians 10:31

The heavens declare the glory of God

Psalm 19:1

In the beginning, God created the heavens and the earth

Genesis 1:1

I praise you God, for I am fearfully and wonderfully made

Psalm 139:14

DO NOT BE AFRAID FOR I AM WITH YOU

ISAIAH 43:5

He is not here, he is risen!

Matthew 28:6

pray without ceasing

1 Thessalonians 5:17

we
love
because
he
first
loved
us

1 John 4:19

BE STILL,

AND KNOW

THAT

I AM GOD

PSALM 46:10

The Lord

gives

wisdom

Proverbs 2:6

Let everything

that

has breath

praise

the LORD!

Psalm 150:6

Fear God

and

keep his

commandments

Ecclesiastes 12:13

Trust in the Lord

forever,

for

the Lord God

is

an everlasting

rock

Isaiah 26:4

Do not

be deceived:

God is not
mocked,

for whatever

one sows,

that will

he also reap

Galatians 6:7

The LORD

is

good

to all

Psalm 145:9

Believe on the Lord Jesus Christ, and you will be saved

Acts 16:31

The LORD knows the way of

the righteous, the wicked will perish

Psalm 1:6

And
do not

grieve

the Holy Spirit

Ephesians 4:30

This is

love for God:

to obey

his commands

1 John 5:3

Made in the USA
Coppell, TX
19 May 2025

49632619R00020